Historic Florida:
Beloved Maitland & Eatonville
"Better Together" Walking Tour

Text copyright ©2024 by John Beacham
ISBN: 979-889546498-4

Editor: Dr. Beth Landa,
Dr. Scot French

Illustrator: Keith Thomas

Published by LOAMC publishing
(Life of a Military Child) ™

Historic Dates

1526: **Portugal** completed first transatlantic slave voyage to Brazil. Other Europeans soon followed. Slaves were regarded as cargo to be sold to work.

1776: United States is formed. By 1819, 11 states were slave states, 11 were free states.

1819: **Missouri** applied for admission as a slave state, tipping the balance of power and elevating the slavery issue. Note: Mark Twain's relatives in Missouri owned slaves.

1850's: Continued westward expansion forced the issue of slavery to the forefront of American politics. Northern antislavery leaders continued their struggle. Many Northerners felt that Southern slaveholders were determined to rule the nation, widening the gap between North and South.

1860: Abraham Lincoln, a known opponent of slavery, was elected president on November 6, and inaugurated on March 4, 1861.

1860: Perceiving a threat, Southern states began seceding from the union in December.

1861: Southern states created **Confederate States of America** with **Jefferson Davis** elected president.

The vice president of the Confederate States of America, **Alexander H. Stephens,** claimed in the Savannah Republican on March 21, 1861 that, "...*its corner–stone rests upon the great truth, that the negro is not equal to the white man; that slavery — subordination to the superior race — is his natural and normal condition.*" **Civil War** breaks out April 15, 1861 after Confederates in Charleston, South Carolina fired on Union-held Fort Sumter

1863: **Emancipation Proclamation** signed by Lincoln on January 1, freeing all slaves.

1864: Lincoln re-elected president.

1865: **Civil War ends** April 9 - Confederate General Robert E. Lee surrendered to General Ulysses S. Grant at Appomattox Court House, Virginia.

1865: Abraham Lincoln was assassinated April 14.

1865: **Freedmen's Bureau Acts of 1865 and 1866** enacted to provide food, shelter, clothing, medical services, and land to displaced Southerners, including the four million newly freed African Americans.

1865: **Thirteenth Amendment** to the United States Constitution ratified on December 18 - providing that "Neither slavery nor involuntary servitude, except as a punishment for crime whereof the party shall have been duly convicted, shall exist within the United States, or any place subject to their jurisdiction."

1868: **Fourteenth Amendment** - granted citizenship to all persons "born or naturalized in the US," including formerly enslaved people, and provided all citizens with "equal protection under the laws," extending the provisions of the Bill of Rights to the states.

Maitland Historic Dates

1838: Fort built along Lake Maitland for use as a stockade during the Seminole War, named in memory of West Point graduate from New York, **William Seton Maitland**.

1842: Fort abandoned. Homesteaders began arriving the following year.

1870's: Post-Civil War, Union veterans and others relocated along the shores of Lake Maitland. There was much work to do, clearing the land, building the homes, and planting the citrus groves. Much of this labor was hired out to "Freedmen," newly emancipated African Americans.

1885: Town of **Lake Maitland** was officially established with the assistance of freedmen. Without the freedmen, there weren't enough male signatures to incorporate the town.

Eatonville Historic Dates

1870's-1880's: Freedmen lived and worked in Lake Maitland, with many living around the shores of **St. John's Hole** in tents and shanty huts (today's Lake Lily). Despite having steady jobs and savings, these Freedmen faced difficulties procuring large enough tracts of land to form an all-black town that could offer them the civil protection they needed.

1881: First black church, St. Lawrence A.M.E. Original church building remains standing (just barely) on Kennedy Ave. Gifted by Northerner and Founding Father Judge Lewis Lawrence to help provide a solid foundation for the new town.

1887: First all-black town in America, **Eatonville,** was officially chartered with the help of Northern Abolitionists living or wintering in Lake Maitland. Today it is one of the few remaining all-black towns. In the 20th century the number of black towns established during segregation has dwindled from a high of 800 in 1920 to only 12 left in 1998. Of those, only about 8 are still in existence today.

1998: Eatonville designated a **National Historic Place** by the National Park Service of the United States Department of the Interior.

Tour Stops:

1. **St. John's Hole** (Lake Lily) – This lake was used by freedmen and their families as a watering hole for laundering clothes. There was year-round work nearby at Lake Maitland but the freedmen lived in shanty shacks around St. John's Hole until a few Maitland residents helped them purchase their own land.

2. **Site of Lawrence Orange Groves** – Site of Copper Rocket today. The grove owner, **Lewis Lawrence**, was a Northern abolitionist who wintered in Lake Maitland and became one of Eatonville's Founding Fathers.

   In 1881 Lawrence purchased over one hundred acres of land from Captain **Josiah Eaton**, another Founding Father, for the purpose of helping to establish an all-black town for the freedmen. Acres were parceled out to black families for purchase on easy terms.

3. **Church of the Good Shepherd** – 331 Lake Av, Maitland. Formed in 1883 by Reverend Henry B. Whipple of Minnesota. In the 1870's his wife advocated building a church for the freedmen who were buying land from Lewis Lawrence in what was to become Eatonville. A stained glass window in the original chapel honors another Founding Father, Captain **Josiah Eaton.**

4. **Thurston House** – 851 Lake Av, Maitland. A Queen Anne Victorian that was built in 1885 by wealthy Minnesotan Cyrus B. Thurston on the shores of Lake Eulalia. The home and lakefront grounds were purchased by the City of Maitland in 1989. Since the 1990's the property, operated by an innkeeper, is the only bed-and-breakfast in Maitland.

5. **Apopka Road** (Kennedy Blvd) – East-West road that started out as a narrow wagon trail. Renamed Kennedy Boulevard after President John F. Kennedy.
   "As a young lad, I watched MLK, JFK and his brother Robert Kennedy all get assassinated. I saw it all play out on the evening news. JFK's famous speech, 'Ask not what your country can do for you, ask what you can do for your country' inspired me to have a servant heart." -John Beacham

6. 1887 Town Charter Plaque – In one plaque, former slave Joseph E. Clark is noted for his role as Town Father.

7. **St. Lawrence A.M.E. Church** – Named after Founding Father **Lewis Lawrence**. Today's church sits on the first ten acres of land purchased by Lewis Lawrence and freedman Joe Clark, and it continues to serve the community today. It is thought to be the first property ever procured for the purpose of establishing a new black town in Florida. In 1936, neighboring Maitland artist Andre Smith, of the Maitland Art Center, donated murals to this church.

8. **Thomas House** – This is the original church building constructed in 1881 that was suggested by Reverend Whipple's wife. It originally stood on the current church site, but it was rolled across the street in 1900 after being outgrown and replaced.

9. **Joe Clark's Store** – Town Father Joe Clark's general store, which carried groceries and general merchandise, was located on the main road in the center of town. (It has been replaced by another building today.) The store's front porch was immortalized by novelist Zora Neale Hurston, who dubbed it, "The Lying Porch" because of all the tall tales that were shared there.

10. Hurston Home Site – Writer Zora Neale Hurston is Eatonville's most acclaimed citizen. She was a prominent Harlem-Renaissance-era novelist, folklorist, and cultural anthropologist who grew up across the street from Joe Clark's general store, thus exposing her to Southern black folklore and culture.

In Zora's memoire, "Dust Tracks on a Road" (1942), she states, *"White Maitland and Negro Eatonville, have lived side by side for fifty-five years without a single instance of enmity. The spirit of the founders has reached beyond the grave."*

Note: John Beacham's Uncle Homer Hamilton (Pie-Pie) was married to Zora's aunt.

Tour Stops - Continued on Page 11

NO TRESPASSING
PROPERTY OF THE
SCHOOL BOARD OF
ORANGE COUNTY,
FLORIDA
LAND
BACK
Historical Hungerford Property
Info@Eatonville1887.com
Eatonville 1887
1887
EATONVILLE FL

BELOVED MAITLAND & EATONVILLE
"Better Together"
WALKING TOUR

1. ST JOHN'S HOLE (Lake Lily)
2. LAWRENCE ORANGE GROVES
3. GOOD SHEPHERD CHURCH
4. THURSTON HOUSE (B & B)
5. APOPKA ROAD (Kennedy Blvd)
6. 1887 TOWN CHARTER PLAQUE
7. ST LAWRENCE A.M.E. CHURCH
8. THOMAS HOUSE (1881 Church Moved)
9. JOE CLARKE'S STORE
10. HURSTON HOME SITE
11. MOSELEY HOUSE
12. CLUB EATON
13. BEN SMITH HOTE
14. MURALS (Lemon
15. MISSIONARY BAP
16. WATER TOWER
17. HURSTON MUSEU
18. HUNGERFORD SC
19. MAITLAND ART &

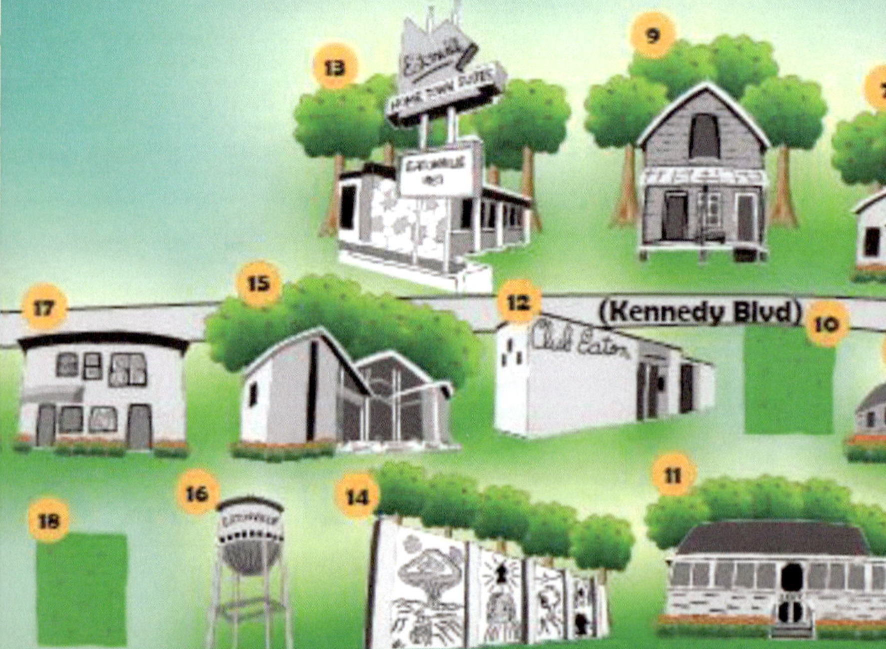

N
LAKE SYBELIA
19
MAITLAND AVE
RCH
OPERTY
MUSEUMS
1
ST. JOHN'S HOLE
(Lake Lily)
LAKE CATHERINE
17-92
6
4
3
KA ROAD
5
2
(Lake Ave)

Eatonville Homeboy Story

By John Beacham

No matter where you walked, everyone shared their wisdom with you, from the old guys sitting on the street corner or sitting in front of the Reed store telling wise tells, or as Zora Neale Hurston, a famous local writer, called them, folklores, or just plain unbelievable lies. But to the Beacham boys it had to be true because most of the stories were told by this older man that everyone called "Homeboy", and boy, could he tell them stories.

When Homeboy told the adult version of his stories, he would run us off by saying, "Do Beacham know you boys are up here?" We always used the same old line, "Yes sir." He would rush us off by grabbing his knife out of his pocket of the same dirty pants he wore every day. Homeboy would say, "Come here you Beachie boys, let me cut your toes off, you don't need them", and we would run and couldn't wait tell our dad when he came home from work that old man Homeboy said he was going to cut our toes and fingers off, because we wanted our dad to go take care of Homeboy:). But that never happened because they were friends.

Eatonville's Clubs

By John Beacham

Inside the walls of the historic township, we gave our nightclubs and our town the nicknames Hooterville USA, and 'The Ville' for Eatonville. As a kid growing up, we called the world-famous Rainbow Nightclub, University of Rainbow USA. Club Eaton was where all the black entertainers came to play, including James Brown, BB King, and Aretha Franklin, because of segregation and safe travel at the time. Club Eaton was called 'The University Club Eaton' because college wasn't in view as a child.

Growing up Eatonville
By John Beacham

Growing up Eatonville with a 3rd grade graduate for a dad, and a mom from the Maitland/Eatonville "Bellamy" family that had enough land to feed Eatonville, you grow up with wisdom at an early age, with the ability to work hard and not make a lot of excuses, because it wasn't allowed, and God was the head of the family.

There was no fear of the outside world, except for what I saw on TV during the civil rights movement and marches, or stories I would overhear from my parents and uncles and neighbors talking about how bad they were treated outside the walls of Eatonville. As I look back, being in an all-Black township had advantages during segregation. Hate was never taught around the house. There was love for each other, and Sunday church was a must.

Being in an all-Black township as a kid you didn't think about the words "can't do it". My father always told us that his dad. our grandfather, killed the word "can't", and he assured us it was dead. It's what I believe today and what I have shared with my kids: there's no such thing as "can't". That's how us Beacham boys and girls have always lived our lives. We believe that if there's a will, there's a way.

Love was served at every meal, especially at breakfast before school, as we walked out the door heading to school. My mom would say, "You're somebody John, Booker, Tim and Sylvester." She would tell us all, "You're a man of dignity, a man of valor." She would add some wisdom into the mix: "Remember, when someone talks to you, look them in their eyes and hold your head up."

I have always believed it to be true, mainly to please my parents, and it gave me so much confidence. I knew I wasn't the smartest kid in my class, but that didn't bother me because I always gave my best and that seemed good enough for the teacher and my parents. Plus, I knew I was loved by my parents, and having so many brothers, I've always had a friend and plenty of great neighbors.

Scot A. French, Ph.D. Associate Professor of History

John Beacham, Founder & Chief Storyteller, Preserve History of Maitland & Eatonville, Inc.

11. **Moseley House** – Original home constructed circa 1888. Tillie Moseley, the childhood best friend of writer Zora Neale Hurston, lived here. Tillie was also a niece of Town Father Joseph E. Clark.

12. **Club Eaton** – Mid-century Eatonville - Big band greats like Duke Ellington and Cab Calloway, blues man B.B. King, and rhythm and blues king James Brown performed at Ben Smith's Club Eaton during its heyday in the 1950's and 1960's.

13. **Ben Smith Motel** – This motel provided safe lodging for Club Eaton's black entertainers during segregation.

14. **Murals** – Ball park murals

15. **Missionary Baptist Church** – 412 East Kennedy Boulevard. The historic Macedonia Missionary Baptist Church has grown in size from its humble beginnings in 1882. It is now one of the largest buildings in Eatonville. Initially the Baptist Church shared quarters with the Methodist Church for a few years. Later in 1889 they purchased a house on Eaton Street for services. By 1895 a much larger church was constructed on the corner of Calhoun Avenue and Apopka Road. In 1902 Zora's father John Hurston became the third pastor, for a period of fifteen years. The present building was completed in 1994.

16. **Water Tower** – Commemorated by a plaque

17. **Hurston Museum** – Established in 1990, this museum features fine art exhibits year-round, and serves as home base for the annual Zora! Festival, a celebration of the arts and humanities, held every January in Eatonville since 1989.

18. **Hungerford School Property** – Booker T. Washington of the Tuskegee Institute in Alabama assisted Eatonville in the establishment of an academy to educate black children. In 1899, Professor Russell C. Calhoun and his wife Mary set up the school, named the Robert Hungerford Normal and Industrial School, to teach vocational, literacy and life skills. The land was donated by E.C. Hungerford for educational purposes.

    Both the original school and a subsequent school on the site have been torn down, and the land is currently vacant. Eatonville has a clear vision for the property – to build cultural, heritage and art sites there and to actively promote historic preservation tourism.

19. **Maitland Art and History Museums** – Designed in the early 1900's by Andre Smith, painter, etcher, author and architect, as an artist colony which he called The Research Studio. Smith designed the 22-building campus in an Aztec-Mayan motif. He was friendly with Eatonville writer Zora Neale Hurston. The lives and communities of blacks in central Florida were a favorite subject for Smith. The present-day museum complex opened in 1971.

    It was in this museum that John Beacham viewed a new exhibit on Eatonville history a few years ago. As he glanced up at a picture on the wall, he exclaimed, "Hey, those are my grandparents, Wes and Gussie!" The curator, Dr. Scot French, a local historian and UCF professor, happened to be present, heard him and thus began a beautiful friendship and collaboration.

Historic Florida: Beloved Community, the Story of Maitland, and Historic Eatonville, "Better Together" Walking Tour

Central Florida's town of Maitland was incorporated two decades after the Civil War with the help of freedmen, and historic Eatonville, the first all-black town in America, was chartered two years later with the help of Maitland citizens. Enjoy this window into some little-known Florida history, presented by authentic speaker John Beacham, whose freedmen ancestors lived it. The two neighboring towns have benefited for 137 years from mutual support. Learn how this amicable relationship evolved, who the heroes are, and which cultural superstars entertained in or emerged from the small town of Eatonville. Come hear the story and gain more insight into the historic events that transpired, not too long ago, in Central Florida.

In the mid-1800's settlers began arriving in and around Lake Maitland. A few years after the Civil War, which ended in 1865, several Union officer veterans colonized the Lake Maitland area. There was plenty of land that needed clearing, homes that needed building, and citrus crops that needed planting and reaping. Many of the local workforce were freedmen, who were ex-slaves or descendants.

With year-round work available, the freedmen were able to earn a good living, but were unable to secure homesteads of their own. All that changed when Eatonville's three founding fathers, freedman Joseph E. Clark, northern abolitionist Lewis Lawrence, and Captain Josiah Eaton, joined forces to help create an all-black town in which freedmen could live, worship, self-govern, and raise and educate a family.

Eatonville1887.com
info@eatonville1887.com

20240418

About the Author

Early Life and Education: **John Beacham** was born in the heart of Florida, where the vibrant culture and rich history of the region shaped his early years. Growing up in a community that celebrated its African American heritage, he developed a profound appreciation for the stories and struggles of those who came before him. Inspired by his family's commitment to community service, John pursued a career in the United States Army, which laid the groundwork for his future endeavors in activism and community development for both veterans and the historic town of Eatonville.

Founding Eatonville 1887: In 2020, John Beacham founded Eatonville 1887, a walking tour initiative designed to celebrate the historical significance of Eatonville, Florida, one of the first incorporated African American municipalities in the United States. Through meticulously curated tours, John aimed to educate both locals and tourists about Eatonville's rich legacy, including its connection to literary figures like Zora Neale Hurston. His passion for storytelling and history transformed the tours into a platform for cultural appreciation and community pride.

Community Development and Activism: John's commitment to Eatonville extended beyond tourism. Recognizing the economic challenges faced by the community, he dedicated himself to creating opportunities for residents. Over the years, John successfully raised over $20 million to support various community projects and events, ranging from educational programs to local festivals. His efforts not only revitalized the local economy but also fostered a sense of unity among residents. In June 2024, John was honored with the title of Community Ambassador, a testament to his unwavering dedication to the people of Eatonville. This accolade recognized his tireless work in advocating for equality, social justice, and community empowerment.

Land Back Movement: In a groundbreaking move that garnered national attention, John Beacham coined the term "Land Back," a movement aimed at addressing historical injustices faced by marginalized communities, particularly in Eatonville. This initiative sought to reclaim cultural heritage and promote equitable access to land and resources. John's vision was to empower residents to take an active role in shaping their community's future while addressing the systemic disadvantages that had persisted for generations. As an equality activist, John Beacham became a leading voice in the fight for social justice, advocating for policies that would uplift and support the residents of Eatonville. His work resonated with many, drawing attention to the unique challenges faced by historically marginalized communities across the nation.

Legacy and Impact: John Beacham's contributions to Eatonville and the broader community have left an indelible mark on the landscape of Florida. Through his innovative walking tours, community initiatives, and advocacy for equality, he has inspired countless individuals to engage with their heritage and work towards a more equitable future. His efforts remind us that community development is not just about economic growth; it is about fostering a sense of belonging, pride, and empowerment among all residents. As a dedicated activist and community leader, John Beacham continues to pave the way for future generations, ensuring that the stories of Eatonville and its residents are celebrated, remembered, and honored. His journey embodies the spirit of resilience and the power of community, making him a true champion for equality and social justice in Florida and beyond.

Current Board Member/Chair:

- Winter Park YMCA • ADA American Diabetes Association • Maitland Rotary Club, Board Member
- Orlando Area Salvation Army • BB&T Bank of Central Florida
- Conductive Education Center of Florida (CECO) • Victory Cup Initiative, Cofounder and Board Member

ISBN 979-889546498-4

9 798889 546498